BATTLE OF JERiCHO

Activity Book for Beginners

Battle of Jericho Activity Book for Beginners

All rights reserved. By purchasing this Activity Book, the buyer is permitted to copy the activity sheets for personal and classroom use only, but not for commercial resale. With the exception of the above, this Activity Book may not be reproduced in whole or in part in any manner without written permission of the publisher.

Bible Pathway Adventures® is a trademark of BPA Publishing Ltd.

Defenders of the Faith® is a trademark of BPA Publishing Ltd.

ISBN: 978-1-989961-65-0

Author: Pip Reid

Creative Director: Curtis Reid

For free Bible resources including coloring pages, worksheets, puzzles and more, visit our website at:

shop.biblepathwayadventures.com

 Introduction for Parents

Enjoy teaching your children about the Bible with our hands-on *Battle of Jericho Activity Book for Beginners*. Packed with detailed lesson plans, coloring pages, fun worksheets, and puzzles to help educators just like you teach children about the Biblical faith. Includes scripture references for easy Bible verse look-up and a handy answer key for teachers.

Bible Pathway Adventures helps educators teach children about the Biblical faith in a fun and creative way. We do this via our Activity Books, Bible storybooks, and free printable activities – available on our website: www.biblepathwayadventures.com

Thanks for buying this Activity Book and supporting our ministry. Every book purchased helps us continue our work providing free Classroom Packs and discipleship resources to families and missions around the world.

The search for Truth is more fun than Tradition!

Table of Contents

Introduction 3

Lesson One: To the promised land 6
Worksheet: Manna and quail 8
Worksheet: Water from the rock 9
Worksheet: The ten commandments 10
Worksheet: Wilderness life 12
Bible word search puzzle: To the promised land… 13
Worksheet: Tabernacle treasures 14
Worksheet: Spies into Canaan 15
Memory verse coloring page: Deuteronomy 1:8 16
Alphabet worksheet: J is for Joshua 17

Lesson Two: Rahab and the spies 18
Map activity: The Israelites' journey 20
Worksheet: The number two 21
Bible craft: Spy out the city of Jericho! 22
Alphabet worksheet: S is for spy 23
Bible verse puzzle: Who helped the spies? 24
Bible word search puzzle: Escape from Jericho! 25
Worksheet: Flax, flax, flax 26
Worksheet: Let's dry some flax 27
Worksheet: Linen and flax 28
Coloring worksheet: Rahab 29
Worksheet: Trace the words 30
Bible craft: Help the spies escape Jericho 31

Lesson Three: Crossing the Jordan 32
Let's learn Hebrew: Yehoshua 34
Bible word search puzzle: Crossing the Jordan River 36
Labyrinth: Help the Israelites cross the Jordan River 37
Worksheet: Water or land 38
Worksheet: What's my sound? 39
Worksheet: W is for water 40

Worksheet: Duties of a priest	41
Coloring page: Israel crosses the Jordan	42
Bible craft: The priests' feet	43
Worksheet: Ark of the covenant	44
Worksheet: You need a reminder!	45

Lesson Four: Battle instructions 46

Worksheet: I spy!	48
Worksheet: I is for Israel	49
Worksheet: The first Passover	50
Worksheet: Wilderness menu	51
Map activity: God's battle plan	52
Bible activity: Battle instructions	53
Worksheet: Walls of Jericho	54
Worksheet: The number seven	55
Let's learn Hebrew: Shofar	56

Lesson Five: Battle of Jericho 58

Worksheet: Label the Israelite	60
Worksheet: Can you follow instructions?	61
Coloring page: Be strong and of a good courage	62
Worksheet: Courage	63
Banner: Be strong and courageous	64
Bible craft: Make a shofar	65
Bible word search puzzle: Fall of Jericho	66
Worksheet: What's different?	67
Worksheet: Up and down	68
Worksheet: R is for Rahab	69

Crafts & Projects

Bible craft: Let's make a menorah!	71
Bible Flashcards	73
Bible craft: Walls of Jericho	77
Bible craft: Retelling a story	83
Certificate of Award	87
Answer Key	89
Discover more Activity Books!	91

LESSON 1

Lesson Plan
To the promised land

Teacher: _____

Today's Bible passages: Exodus 12, 17, 20, 26, Numbers 13, Deuteronomy 34, and Joshua 1

Welcome prayer:
Pray a simple prayer with the children before you begin the lesson.

Lesson objectives:
In this lesson, children will learn:
1. How God promised the Israelites a new land
2. How God took care of the Israelites in the desert

Did You Know?
Manna tasted like crackers made with honey. The Israelites ate manna for 40 years!

Bible lesson overview:
The Hebrews were slaves in the land of Egypt for many years. But God had promised them a new land - the land of Canaan (Promised Land). God always keeps His promises. After He sent ten plagues on Egypt, Pharaoh told Moses and the Israelites to leave. And so, they left for the land of Canaan. Along the way, God took care of them; He gave them manna and quail to eat, and water to drink. The Israelites lived in the desert where they had many adventures: they stayed in tents and learned the ten commandments, built a tabernacle, and even saw giants! After 40 years, they arrived at the Jordan river. There Moses died and Joshua became the Israelites' new leader.

Let's Review:
Questions to ask your students:
1. What land did God promise the Hebrews?
2. How long did the Israelites live in the desert?
3. What did God give the people to eat and drink?
4. What adventures did the Israelites have in the desert?
5. Who was the Israelites' first leader? After he died, who became the new leader?

 A memory verse to help children remember God's Word:
"Moses led the people out of Egypt…" (Acts 7:36)

Activities:
Worksheet: Manna and quail
Worksheet: Water from the rock
Worksheet: The ten commandments
Worksheet: Wilderness life
Bible word search puzzle: To the promised land…
Worksheet: Tabernacle treasures
Bible craft: Let's make a menorah!
Worksheet: Spies into Canaan
Memory verse coloring page: Deuteronomy 1:8
Alphabet worksheet: J is for Joshua

Closing prayer:
End the lesson with a short prayer.

Manna and quail

The Israelites ate manna and quail in the desert.
How many baskets of manna do you see?
How many quail do you see?
Color the manna yellow. Color the quails blue.

Water from the rock

God gave the Israelites water to drink from a rock (Exodus 17). Glue pieces of blue paper onto the rock to make a waterfall!

The ten commandments

In the desert, God gave the Israelites the ten commandments (Exodus 20:1-17). Read the ten commandments. Color the pictures.

I am Yahweh your God. Do not have other gods

Do not make idols

Do not take the name of God in vain

Remember the Sabbath

Honor your father and mother

Do not murder

Do not commit adultery

Do not steal

Do not lie

Do not want other people's things

Wilderness life

In the desert, the Israelites lived in tents.
Trace the triangles.

Trace and color the hills and tents.

To the promised land...

Find and circle each of the words from the list below.

```
M O S E S T
M A N N A E
M B F Q R N
L A N D O T
H E B R E W
D E S E R T
```

MANNA LAND
TENT   MOSES
DESERT HEBREW

Tabernacle treasures

The Israelites built a tent (a tabernacle) in the desert to worship God. Inside they put special furniture items. Trace a dotted line from each item to the tabernacle. Color the pictures.

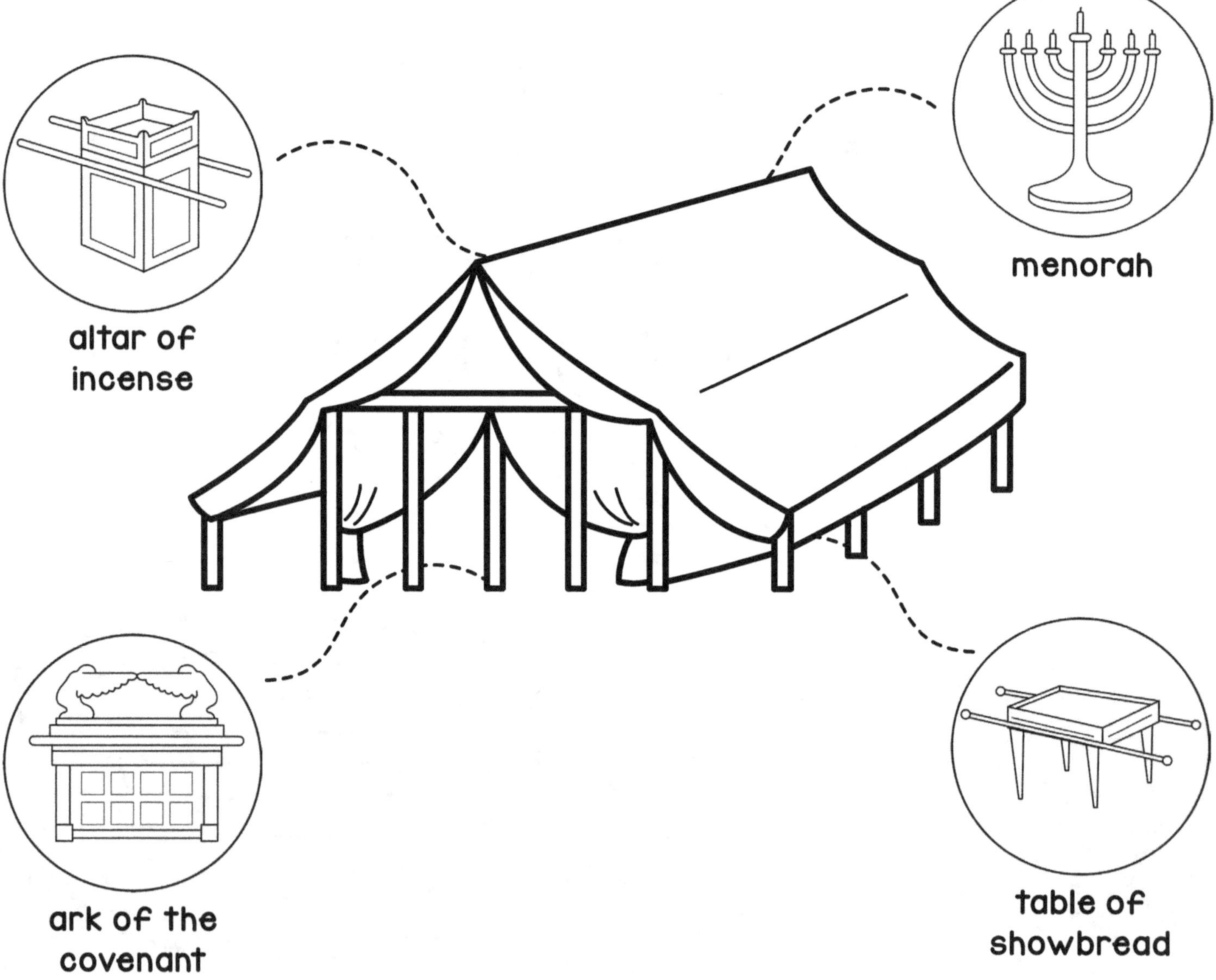

altar of incense

menorah

ark of the covenant

table of showbread

Spies into Canaan

Moses sent 12 spies to see the Promised Land (Numbers 13:1, 26-29). What did they find? Trace the words. Color the pictures.

 Big fruit

 Big cities

 Big people

J is for Joshua

After Moses died, Joshua became the leader of the Israelites (Joshua 1:1-2). Trace the letters. Color the picture.

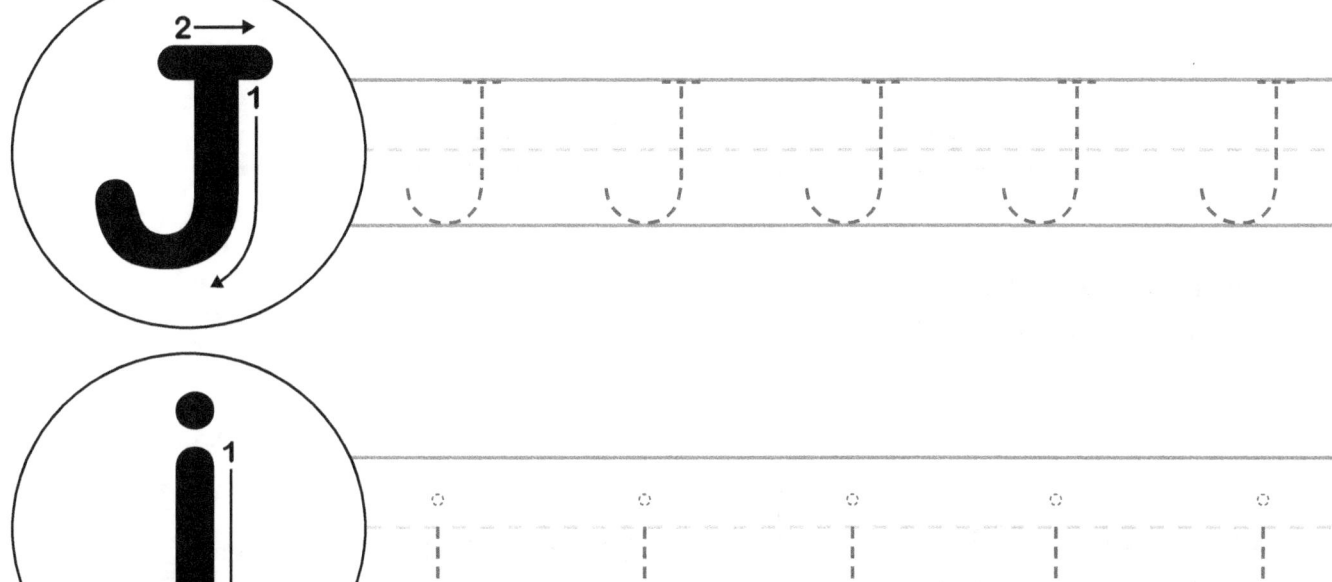

Trace the letter j

Color Joshua

LESSON 2 | Lesson Plan
Rahab and the spies

Teacher: _____

Today's Bible passage: Joshua 2:1-24

 **Welcome prayer:**
Pray a simple prayer with the children before you begin the lesson.

Lesson objectives:
In this lesson, children will learn:
1. Why the king of Jericho was afraid of the Israelites
2. Why the spies promised to protect Rahab

Did You Know?
In Bible times, people slept on the roofs of their houses when the weather was hot.

Bible lesson overview:
The Israelites wanted to attack Jericho. Joshua sent two men (spies) to the city. They stayed at the house of a woman named Rahab. The king of Jericho was scared. He had heard all about the fearsome Israelites. "Find these men!" he said. But Rahab hid the men under stalks of flax on her roof. "If you save me and my family, I will not tell the king's men where you are," she said. The spies agreed to help her family. "Tie a red rope to your window. We will save you when we attack the city." When the king's men came to Rahab's house, she told them the men had gone. Then, Rahab used the red rope to let the men escape. They climbed out the window and went back to the camp to tell Joshua what they had seen.

Let's Review:
Questions to ask your students:
1. Why did Joshua send spies to the city?
2. Who helped the spies hide from the king's men?
3. Where did the spies hide?
4. What special instructions did the spies give Rahab?
5. After the spies escaped the city, where did they go?

 A memory verse to help children remember God's Word:
"Rahab tied the red rope in the window." (Joshua 2:21)

Activities:
Map activity: The Israelites' journey
Worksheet: The number two
Bible craft: Spy out the city of Jericho!
Alphabet worksheet: S is for spy
Bible verse puzzle: Who helped the spies?
Bible word search puzzle: Escape from Jericho!
Worksheet: Flax, flax, flax
Worksheet: Let's dry some flax
Worksheet: Linen and flax
Coloring worksheet: Rahab
Worksheet: Trace the words
Bible craft: Help the spies escape Jericho

 Closing prayer:
End the lesson with a short prayer.

The Israelites' journey

The Israelites left Egypt and headed to the land of Canaan (the Promised Land). Connect the dots to see their journey from Egypt to the Jordan River.

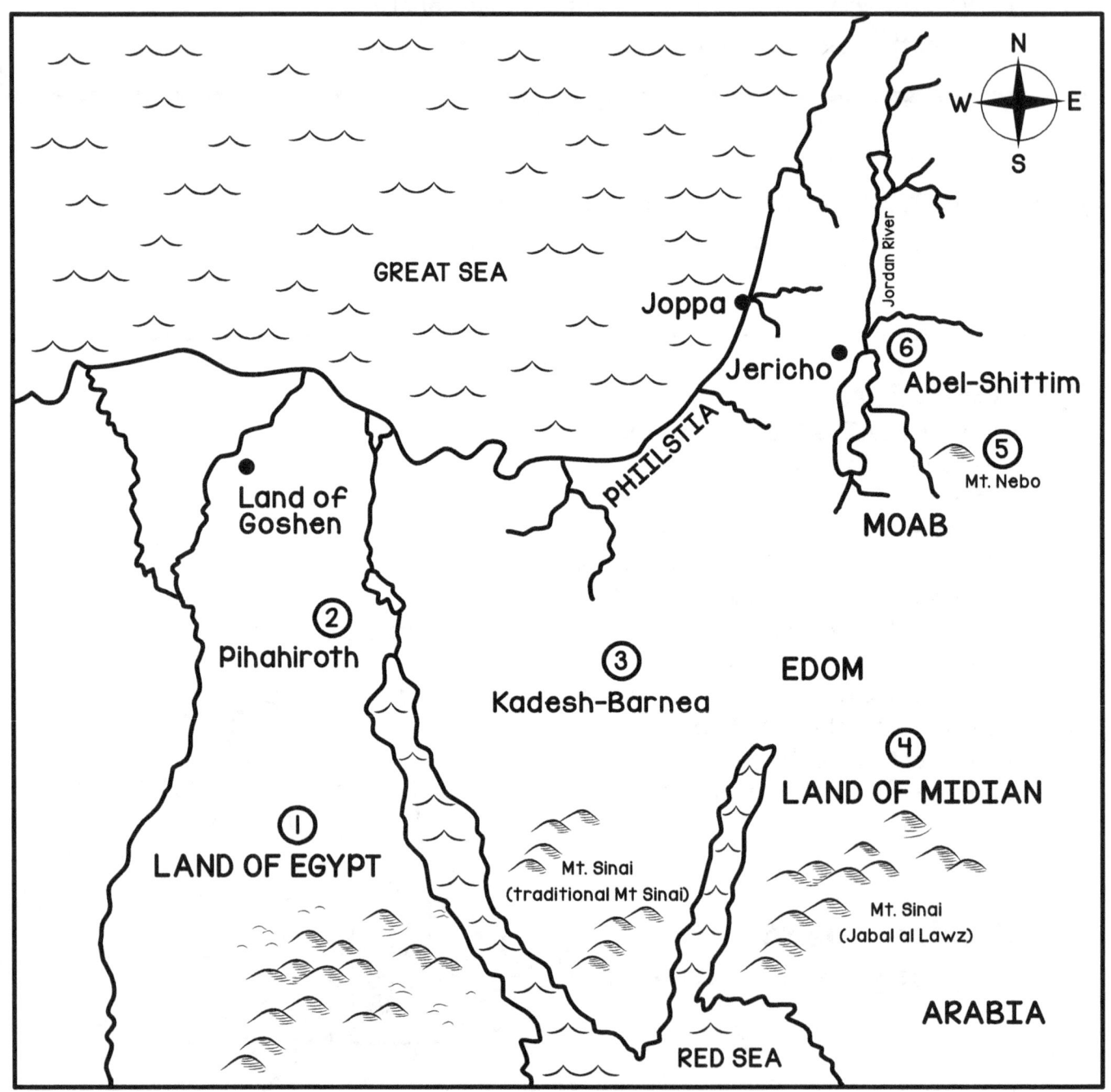

Trace the number two.

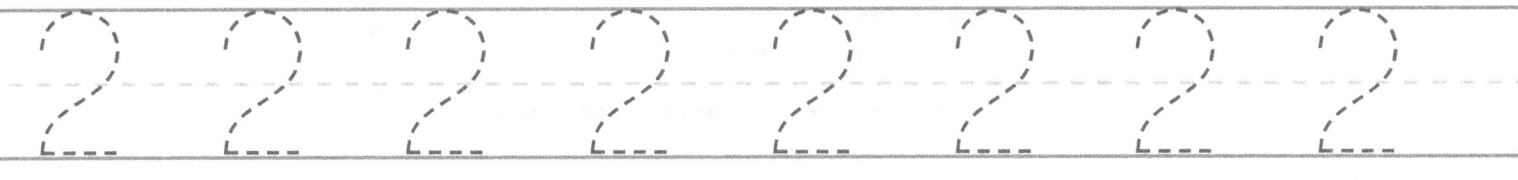

Write the number two in the boxes below.

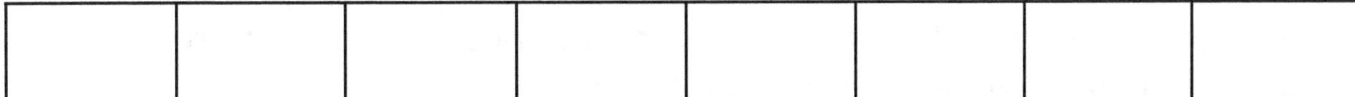

How many fingers are there?

How many spies did Joshua send to Jericho?

....

Spy out the city of Jericho!

You will need:
1. Paper toilet rolls x 2
2. White or colored paper
3. Scissors (adults-only)
4. Felt pens or crayons
5. School glue, tape, or glue stick
6. Hole punch
7. Yarn or string

Instructions:

1. Paste a piece of white or colored paper around each toilet roll.
2. Ask your child to decorate each toilet roll.
3. Tape the two rolls together using a piece of tape at each end.
4. Create a hole in the outer side of each tube. Thread yarn or string through to create a neck strap.

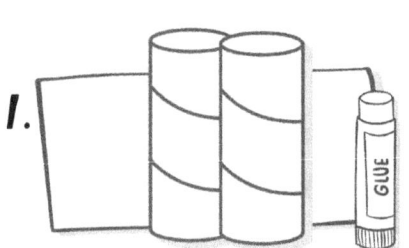
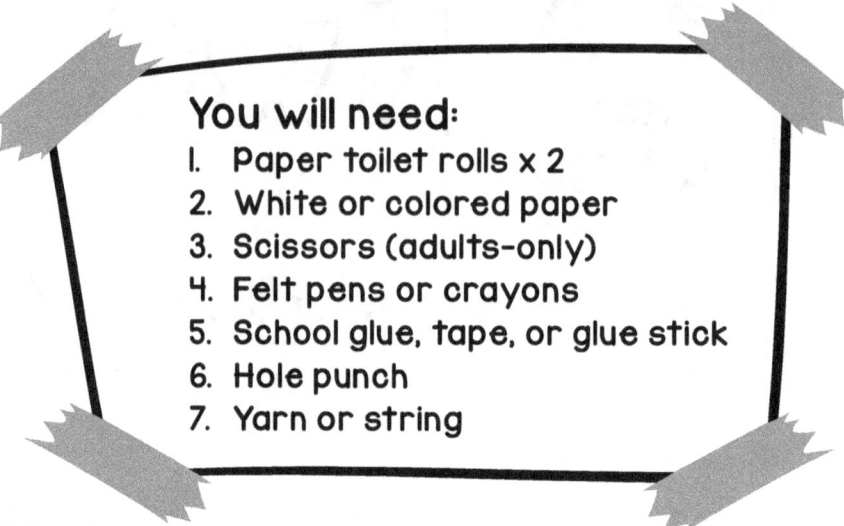
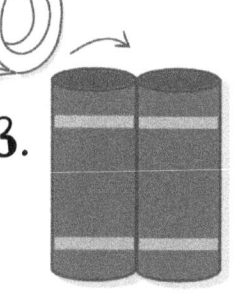

S is for Spy

Joshua sent two spies to the city of Jericho. A spy is a person who watches people in secret, and gets information. Trace the word 'spy'. Circle and color the pictures that start with the letter 's'.

spy

flax

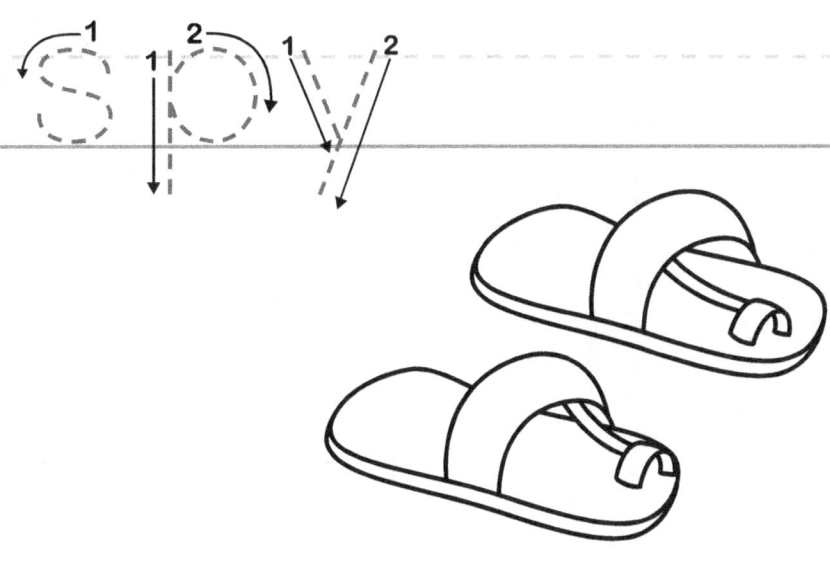
sandals

manna

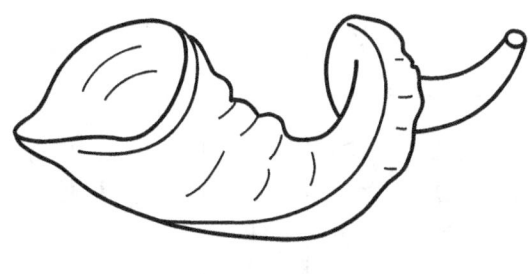
shofar

Who helped the spies?

Fill in the blanks using the chart below.
What do you see?

What is a spy?

__ __ __ __ __
18 1 8 1 2

__ __ __ __ __ __
8 5 12 16 5 4

__ __ __ __ __ __ __ __
20 8 5 19 16 9 5 19

A	B	C	D	E	F	G	H	I	J	K	L	M
1	2	3	4	5	6	7	8	9	10	11	12	13
N	O	P	Q	R	S	T	U	V	W	X	Y	Z
14	15	16	17	18	19	20	21	22	23	24	25	26

Escape from Jericho!

Find and circle each of the words from the list below.

```
F L A X W F
R O P E A C
H S Q N L I
N U Q M L T
S P I E S Y
R A H A B Q
```

RAHAB SPIES
WALL   FLAX
CITY   ROPE

Flax, flax, flax

What a lot of flax! Count the bundles of flax.
Write the number in the box.

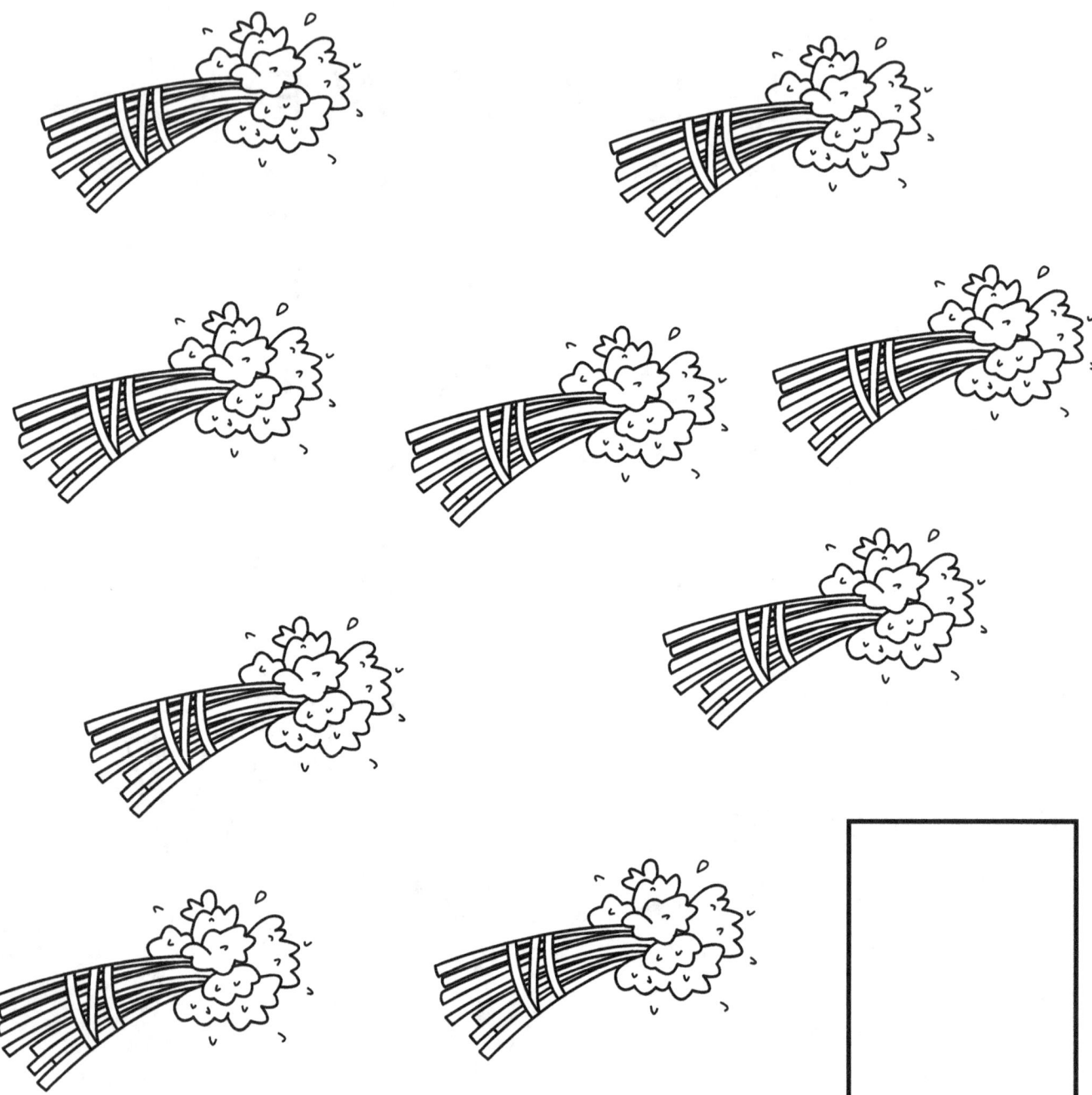

Let's dry some flax

Flax was tied into bundles and dried on wooden racks. Rahab dried flax on her roof. Trace the lines to complete the picture. Color the picture.

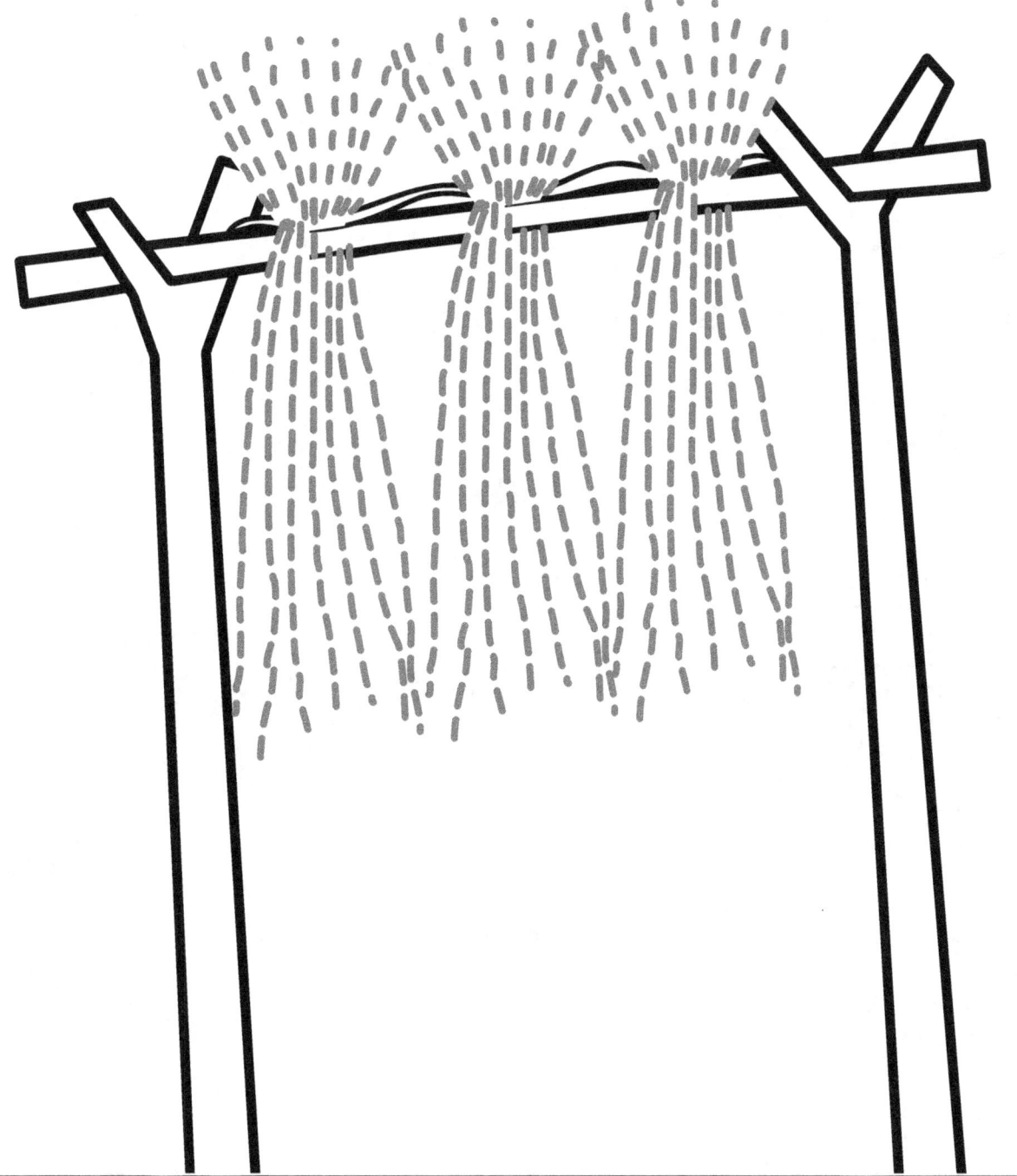

Linen and flax

In Bible times, linen cloth was made from flax plants. People used white linen cloth to wrap dead bodies, make bed sheets, and special clothes for the priests. Flax seeds were used to make oil. Trace the words. Color the pictures.

Priest's clothes

Flax seeds

Bed sheets

White cloth

Trace the words

Color the pictures.

Help the spies escape Jericho

Rahab helped the two spies escape the city. Draw some flax on the roof of the house. Glue a piece of red string or yarn from the window to help the spies escape Jericho. Color the page.

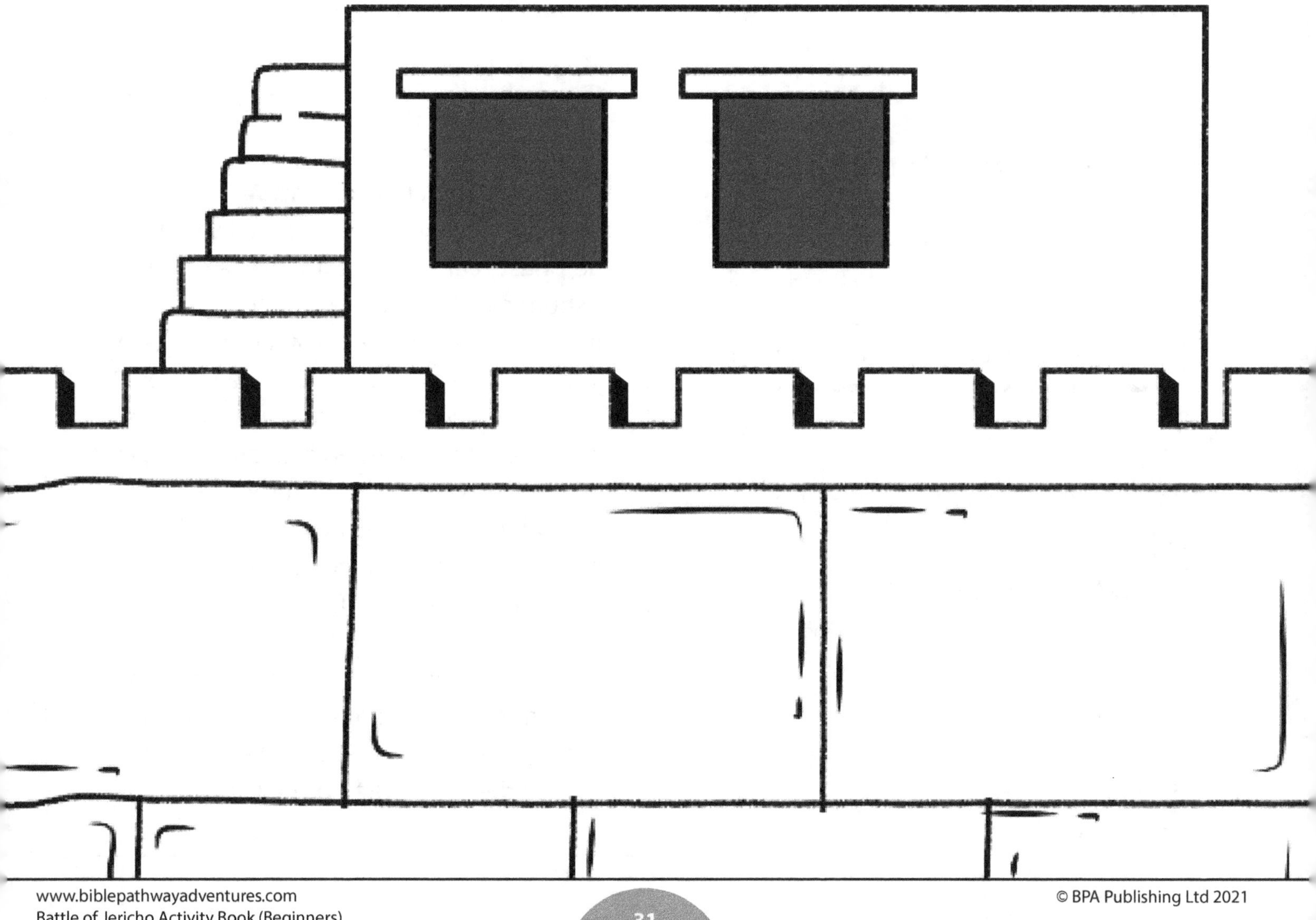

Bible Pathway Adventures

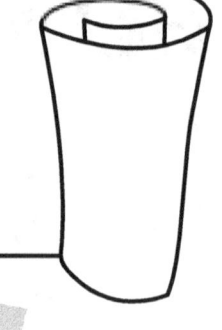

LESSON 3 | Lesson Plan
Crossing the Jordan

Teacher: _____

Today's Bible passage: Joshua 3:1-4:24

 Welcome prayer:
Pray a simple prayer with the children before you begin the lesson.

Lesson objectives:
In this lesson, children will learn:
1. How the Israelites crossed the Jordan River
2. Why Joshua built a stone memorial in the Jordan River

Bible lesson overview:
It was time to cross the Jordan River. "Follow the priests carrying the ark of the covenant," Joshua told the Israelites. "When they enter the water, the river will stop flowing. A dry path will appear and you can walk across." The priests took the ark and went into the river. The waters divided into two parts, and the people walked through the river on a dry pathway. After everyone crossed the river, Joshua told twelve men to take twelve stones from the river. "Put these stones at the place where you will camp," he said. Joshua made another pile of twelve stones in the middle of the river. "Tell your children that these stones will show them where we crossed the river," he told the Israelites.

 **Did You Know?**
The priests were of the tribe of Levi, one of the 12 tribes of Israel.

Let's Review:
Questions to ask your students:
1. Who did Joshua tell the Israelites to follow?
2. Which river did the Israelites cross?
3. How many parts did the waters divide into?
4. Where did the twelve Israelites build a memorial?
5. How many stones did Joshua use to build a memorial?

 A memory verse to help children remember God's Word:
"…all the Israelites walked across the river on dry land." (Joshua 3:17)

Activities:
Let's learn Hebrew: Yehoshua
Bible word search puzzle: Crossing the Jordan River
Labyrinth: Help the Israelites cross the Jordan River
Worksheet: Water or land
Worksheet: What's my sound?
Worksheet: W is for water
Worksheet: Duties of a priest
Coloring page: Israel crosses the Jordan
Bible craft: The priests' feet
Worksheet: Ark of the covenant
Worksheet: You need a reminder!

 **Closing prayer:**
End the lesson with a short prayer.

Yehoshua

The Hebrew name for Joshua is Yehoshua. Joshua was born in the land of Egypt. He helped Moses lead the Israelites through the desert to the Promised Land. Joshua died when he was 110 years old! (Joshua 24:29)

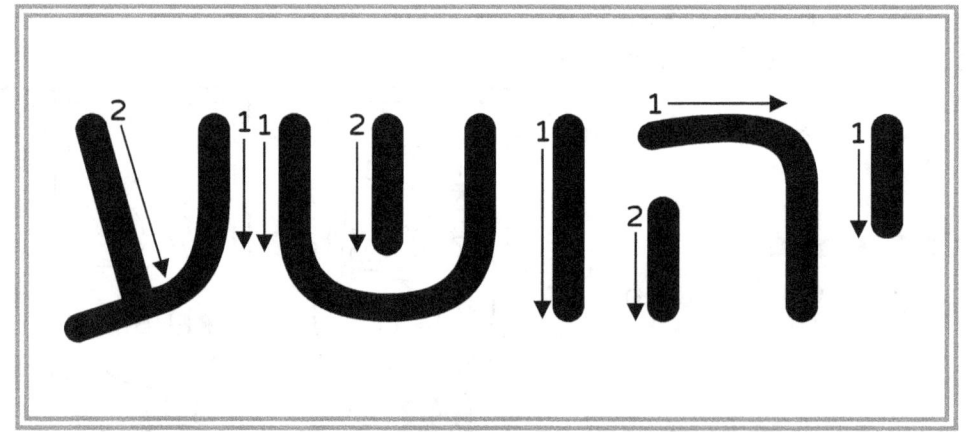

 Let's write!

Write the name Yehoshua on the lines below.

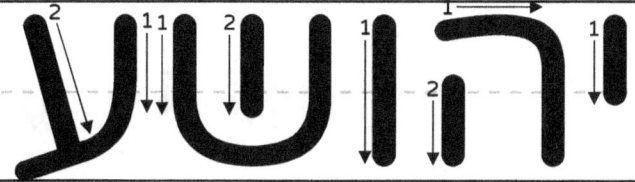

Try this on your own.
Remember that Hebrew is read from RIGHT to LEFT.

🍃 Crossing the Jordan 🍃

Find and circle each of the words from the list below.

```
R I V E R P
R O C K S E
H A V E A O
W A T E R P
L V G L K L
T W E L V E
```

RIVER   ARK
WATER   PEOPLE
ROCKS   TWELVE

Help the Israelites cross the Jordan

God stopped the Jordan River flowing so the Israelites could cross on dry land (Joshua 4:23). Help the Israelites walk across the dry riverbed.

Water or land

The Jordan River is full of water.
What animals live in water? What lives on land?
Draw two pictures in the boxes below.

What's my sound?

The word 'river' starts with the letter R. Circle and color the pictures that have the same beginning sound as river.

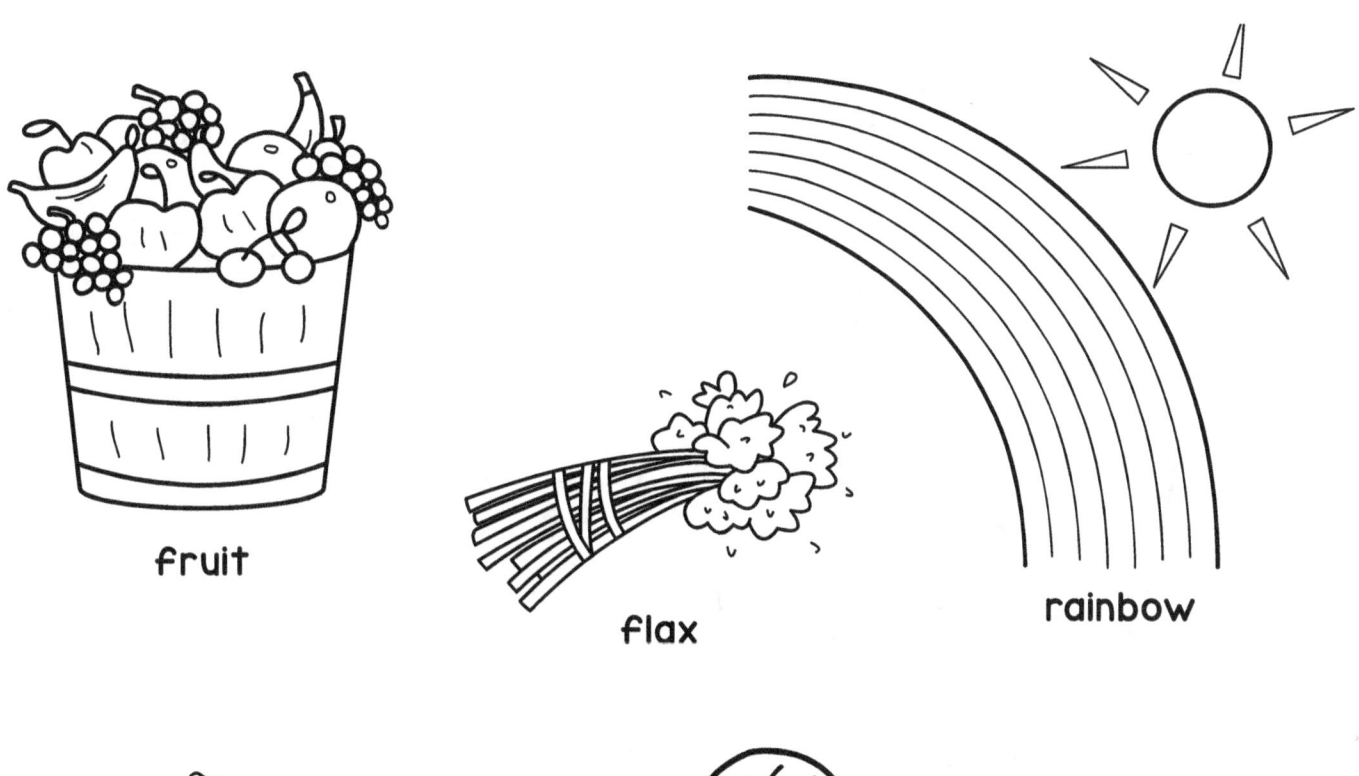

fruit

flax

rainbow

grain

ram

W is for water

is for

water

Duties of a priest

On the way to the Promised Land, God gave the priests many jobs. Can you name some of them? Trace the words. Color the pictures.

Carry the ark

Blow the shofar

Bless Israel

Teach the Torah

I see a priest

"When the feet of the priests carrying the Ark of the Covenant... shall rest in the waters of the Jordan, the waters will stop..."

The priests' feet

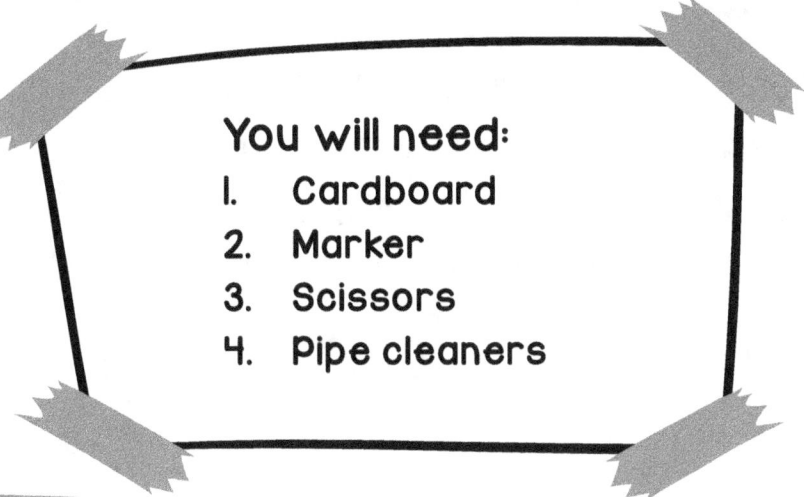

You will need:
1. Cardboard
2. Marker
3. Scissors
4. Pipe cleaners

Instructions:

1. Draw a large foot onto a piece of cardboard and cut it out.
2. Turn it over and trace onto another piece of cardboard, and cut out. This way you will get a matching left and right foot.
3. Cut four holes into each foot around where your child's foot will go. Thread the pipe cleaners through from the back (two pipe cleaners for each foot).
4. Place your child's feet onto the cardboard feet and fasten with the pipe cleaners.

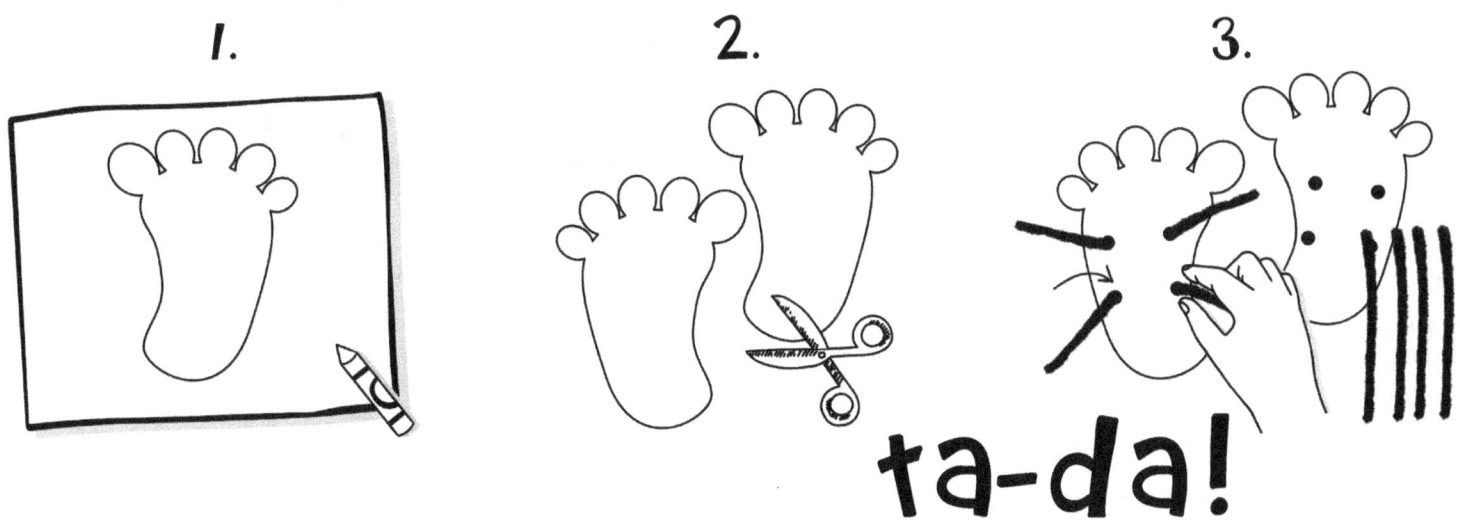

ta-da!

Ark of the covenant

Priests carried the ark of the covenant across the Jordan River. The ark was a special box covered in gold. Read Hebrews 9:4 to learn what was inside the Ark. Trace the squares. Color the ark.

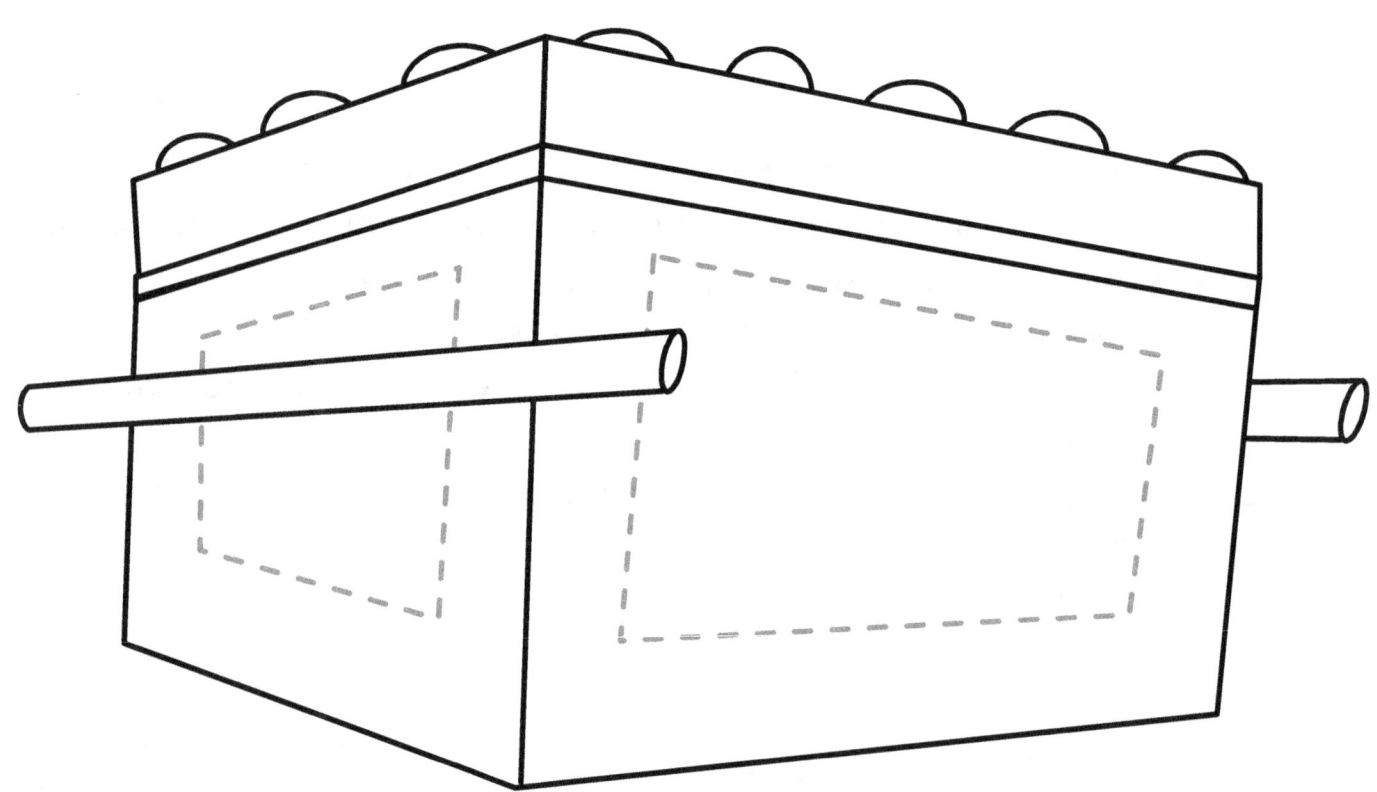

YOU NEED A REMINDER!

After the Israelites crossed the Jordan River, they put 12 rocks at the place where they camped. There was one rock for each tribe of Israel. The rocks reminded the people what God had done. Count the rocks. Trace and color each rock a different color.

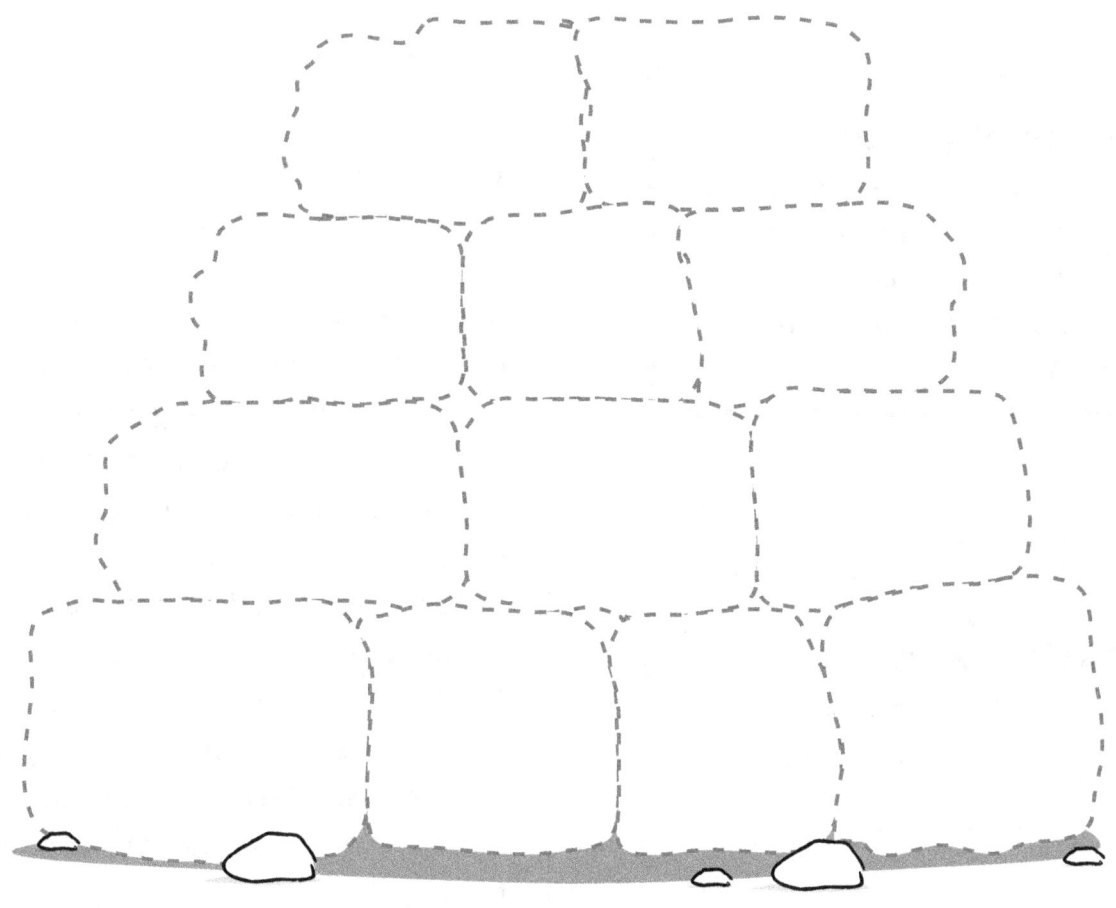

LESSON 4

Lesson Plan
Battle instructions

Teacher: _____

Today's Bible passage: Joshua 5:10–6:7

Welcome prayer:
Pray a simple prayer with the children before you begin the lesson.

Lesson objectives:
In this lesson, children will learn:
1. How the Israelites kept the Passover in Canaan
2. God's battle instructions to Joshua

Did You Know?
The Israelites blew shofars to show a battle was about to start.

Bible lesson overview:
The Israelites camped near the city of Jericho. There, the Israelites ate a Passover meal of lamb and bitter herbs. From that day on, God stopped giving them manna from heaven to eat. They only ate food from the land of Canaan. One day, an angel came to Joshua and told him how to win the battle of Jericho. "March your army around the city once a day for six days. Tell seven priests to walk ahead of the ark, carrying shofars. On the seventh day, march around the city seven times. When you hear the priests blow the shofars, tell the people to shout loudly. The city wall will fall down and you can enter the city."

Let's Review:

Questions to ask your students:
1. What special meal did the Israelites eat?
2. What food did God stopping giving the Israelites to eat?
3. Who appeared to Joshua?
4. How many times did the angel tell the Israelites to march around the city?
5. What did the angel tell Joshua would happen on the seventh day?

 A memory verse to help children remember God's Word:
"You will defeat the king and all the fighting men in the city." (Joshua 6:2)

 ### Activities:

Worksheet: I spy!
Worksheet: I is for Israel
Worksheet: The first Passover
Worksheet: Wilderness menu
Map activity: God's battle plan
Bible activity: Battle instructions
Worksheet: Walls of Jericho
Worksheet: The number seven
Let's learn Hebrew: Shofar
Bible Flashcards

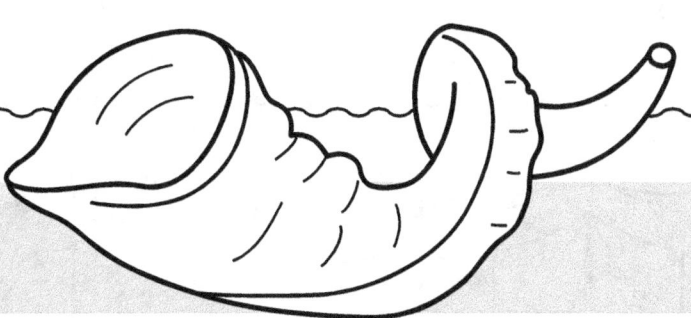

 ### Closing prayer:
End the lesson with a short prayer.

I spy!

The Israelites camped in the wilderness for forty years (Joshua 5:6). Beside the objects below, what else do you think they needed? Color the same objects a single color. Count each object and write the number on the label.

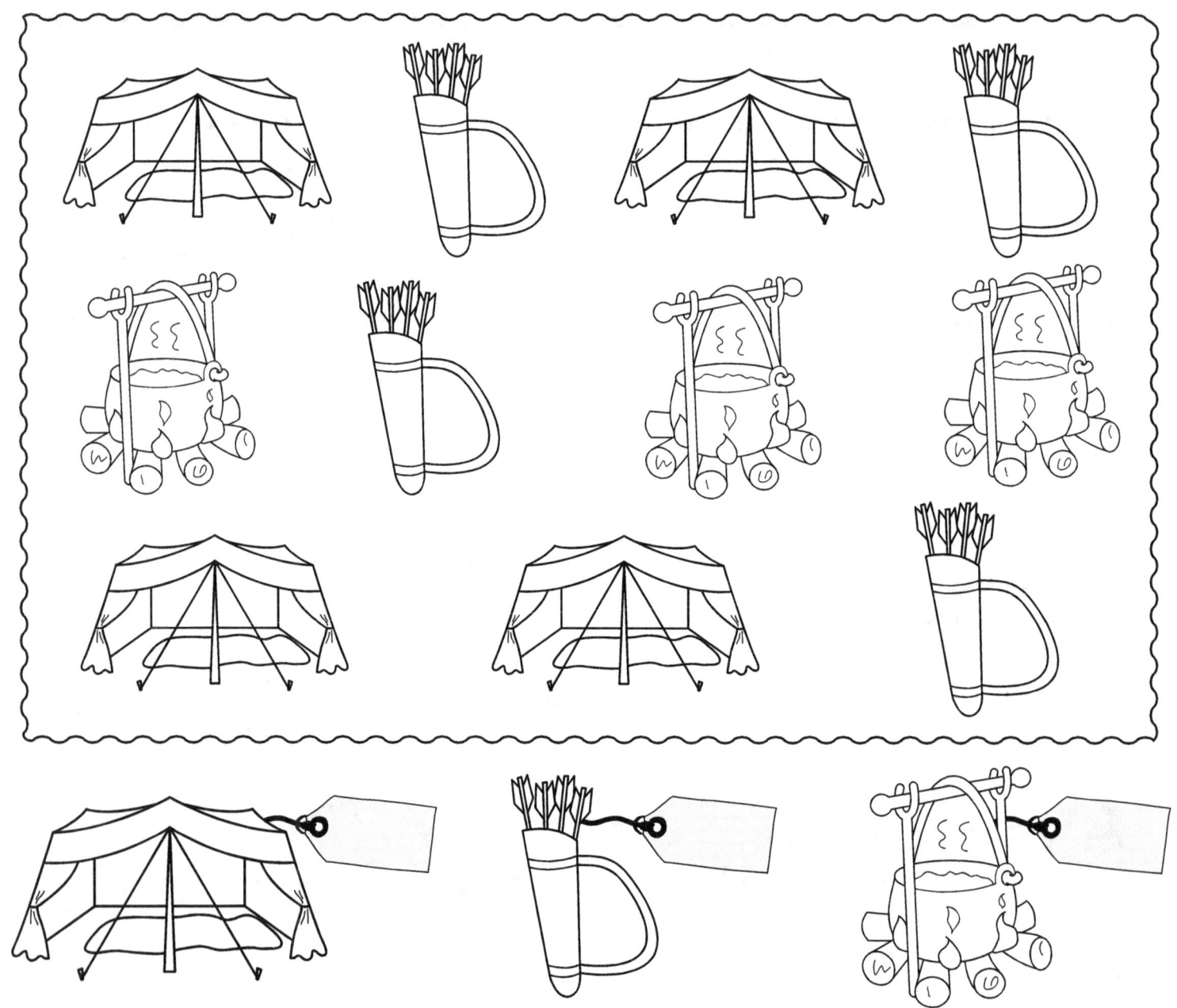

The people of Israel

The people of Israel camped at Gilgal (Joshua 5:10). They ate a Passover meal and got ready for battle. Trace the word 'Israel'. Circle and color the pictures that start with the letter 'I'.

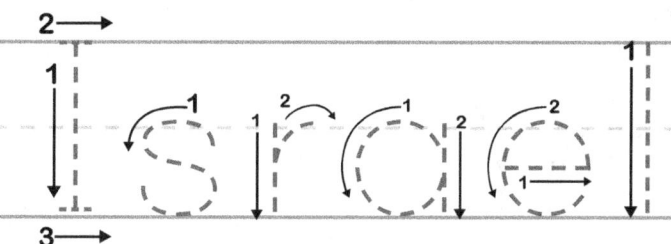

ice cream

insect

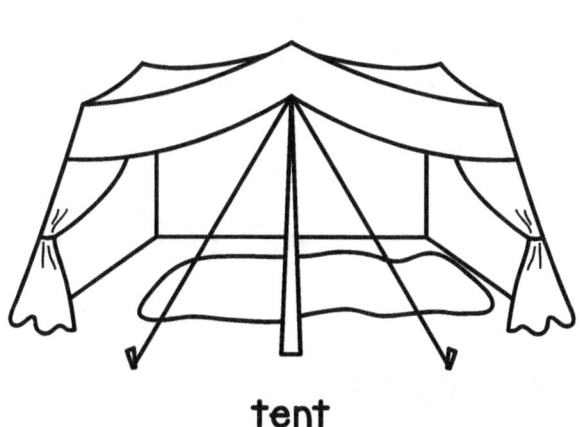
tent

donkey

The first Passover

Parents: Read Exodus 12. Discuss with your child how each picture relates to the Passover. Cut out a word at the bottom of the page. Place it next to the correct picture.

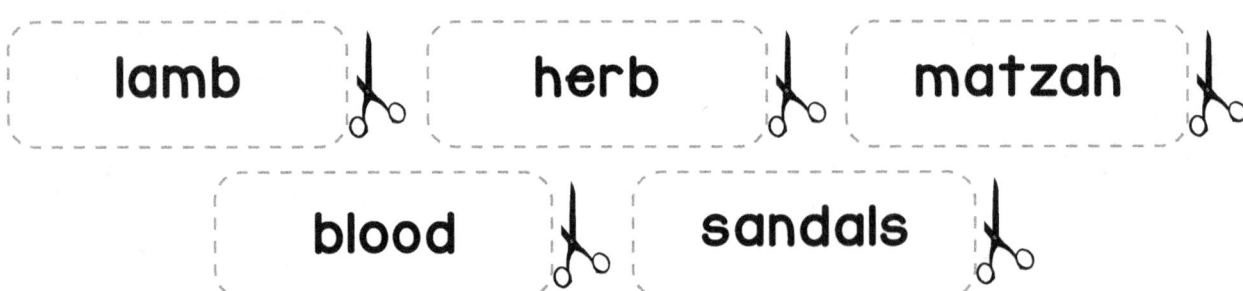

lamb   herb   matzah

blood   sandals

Wilderness menu

Read Joshua 5:10-12. The day after the Passover, God stopped giving the people manna to eat. Instead they ate food from the land of Canaan. Draw an Israelite meal on the plate below.

Circle the food that the Israelites ate in the land of Canaan.

God's battle plan

The commander of God's army told Joshua how to defeat the city of Jericho. Connect the dots to see the Israelites' journey to Jericho.

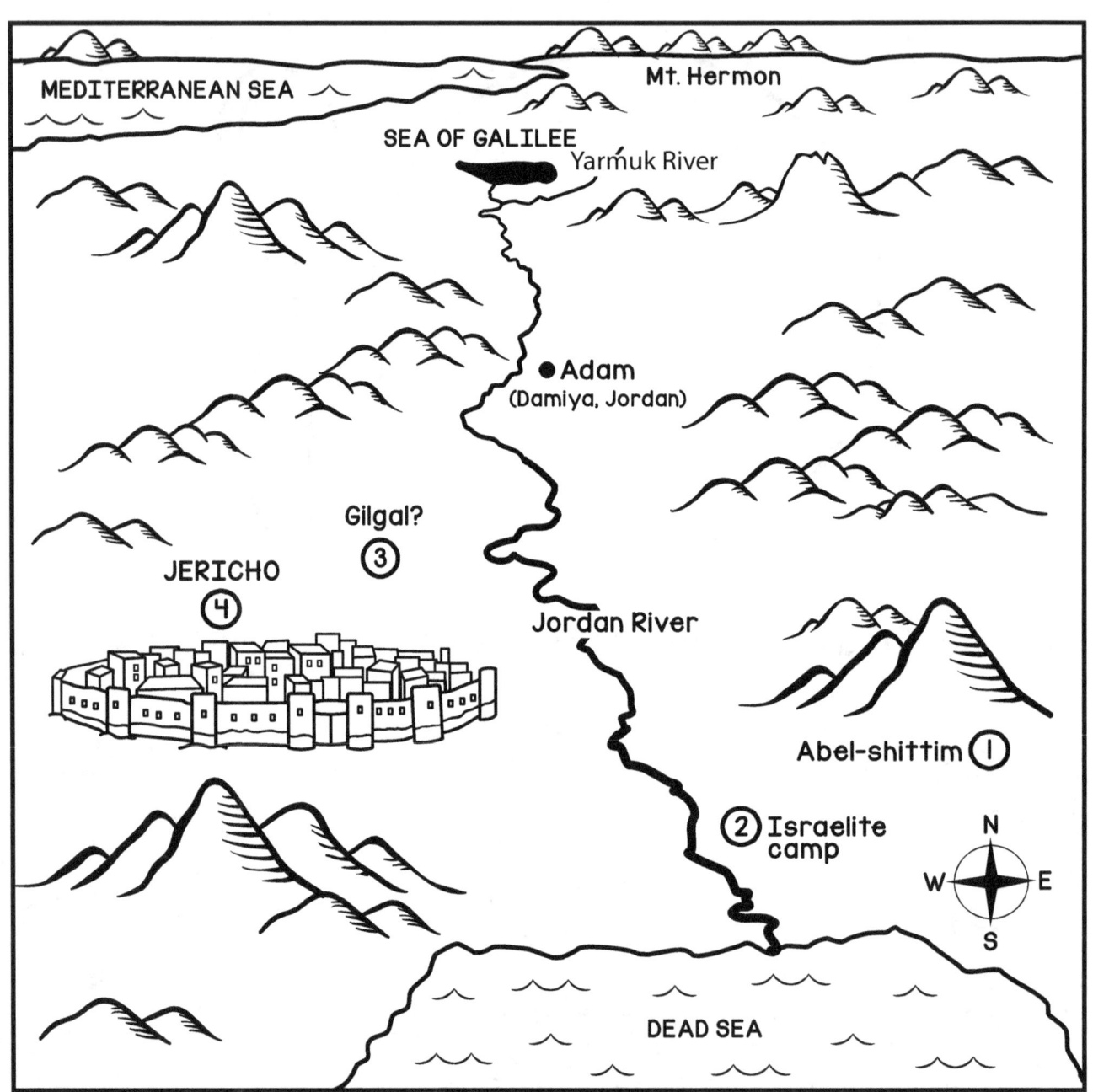

Battle instructions

(Joshua 6:1-20)

Let's march march march
(children march in place)

Around the wall
(children march in a circle)

On the seventh day
(children hold up seven fingers)

The shofars blow
(children cup mouth and make a trumpet sound)

The wall will fall!
(children crouch down)

🌿 Walls of Jericho 🌿

The city wall was tall.
Read the word. Trace the word.
Write it yourself!

tall

The wall is

Draw some tall objects in your neighborhood.

 seven

A shofar (trumpet) is made from a ram's horn.

Write the number seven in the boxes below.

| | | | | | | | |

How many fingers are there?

Read Joshua 6:6. How many shofars did the priests carry?

....

✶ Shofar ✶

The Hebrew word for trumpet is shofar. A shofar is made from a ram's horn. Joshua told the priests to walk around Jericho and blow the shofars (Joshua 6:6).

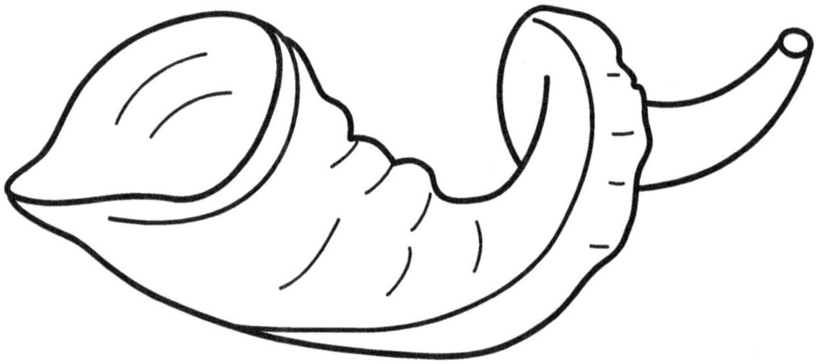

shofar

שׁוֹפָר

trumpet

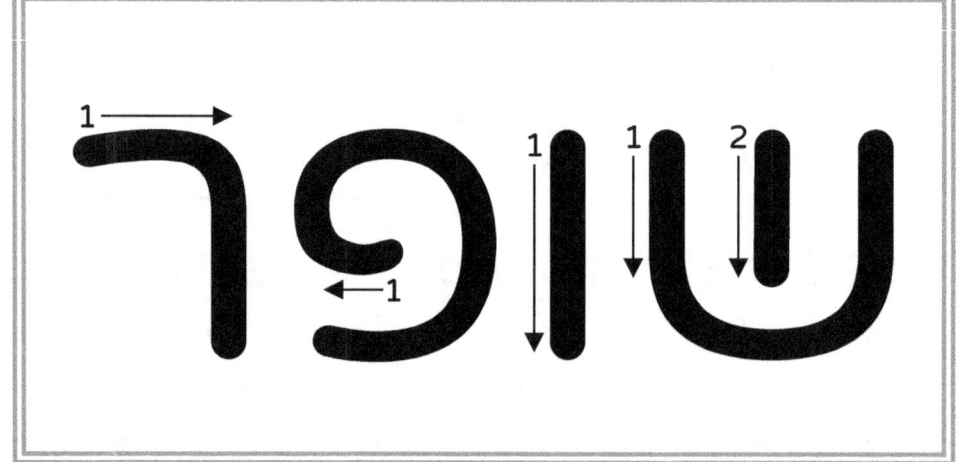

Let's write!

Practice writing this Hebrew word on the lines below.

שׁופר

שׁופר

Try this on your own.
Remember that Hebrew is read from RIGHT to LEFT.

LESSON 5 | Lesson Plan
Battle of Jericho

Teacher: _____

Today's Bible passage: Joshua 6:6-27

 **Welcome prayer:**
Pray a simple prayer with the children before you begin the lesson.

Lesson objectives:
In this lesson, children will learn:
1. How the walls of Jericho fell down
2. How the spies saved Rahab and her family

Did You Know?
Archaeologists found the ruins of ancient Jericho near the Dead Sea.

Bible lesson overview:
It was time to attack the city. Joshua said to the priests, "Take the ark and march around Jericho with your shofars." He told the Israelites, "March around the city. Do this once a day for six days. Do not speak." The Israelites marched around the city wall every day for six days. The priests blew the shofars and the people did not speak. On the seventh day, the Israelites marched around the city seven times. The seventh time around, the priests blew their shofars and the people shouted at the top of their voices. The city wall fell down and the Israelites ran up into Jericho. They burned the city and saved Rahab and her family. God was with Joshua and he became famous everywhere!

Let's Review:

Questions to ask your students:
1. What did Joshua tell the priests to take when they marched around the city?
2. What did Joshua tell the people <u>not</u> to do when they marched around the city?
3. What happened on the seventh day?
4. Who did the two spies save?
5. Was God happy or unhappy with Joshua?

A memory verse to help children remember God's Word:
"Now, shout! God is giving you this city!" (Joshua 6:16)

Activities:
Worksheet: Label the Israelite
Worksheet: Can you follow instructions?
Coloring page: Be strong and of a good courage
Worksheet: Courage
Banner: Be strong and courageous
Bible craft: Walls of Jericho
Bible craft: Make a shofar
Bible word search puzzle: Fall of Jericho
Worksheet: What's different?
Worksheet: Up and down
Worksheet: R is for Rahab
Bible craft: Retelling a story
Certificate of Award

Closing prayer:
End the lesson with a short prayer.

🌿 Label the Israelite 🌿

Use the words in the box to label parts of an Israelite. Color the Israelite.

| sandals | tunic | hair | belt |

Can you follow instructions?

God gave Joshua instructions for the battle of Jericho. Did Joshua listen? How do you know? Listen to your teacher and follow the instructions.

1. Write the letter C on the city.
2. Color the city yellow.
3. Draw a sun in the sky.
4. Color the trees green.
5. Color the ground brown.
6. Draw a cloud in the sky.
7. Color the sky blue.
8. Write your name on the page.

"Be Strong and of a good Courage."

(Joshua 1:9)

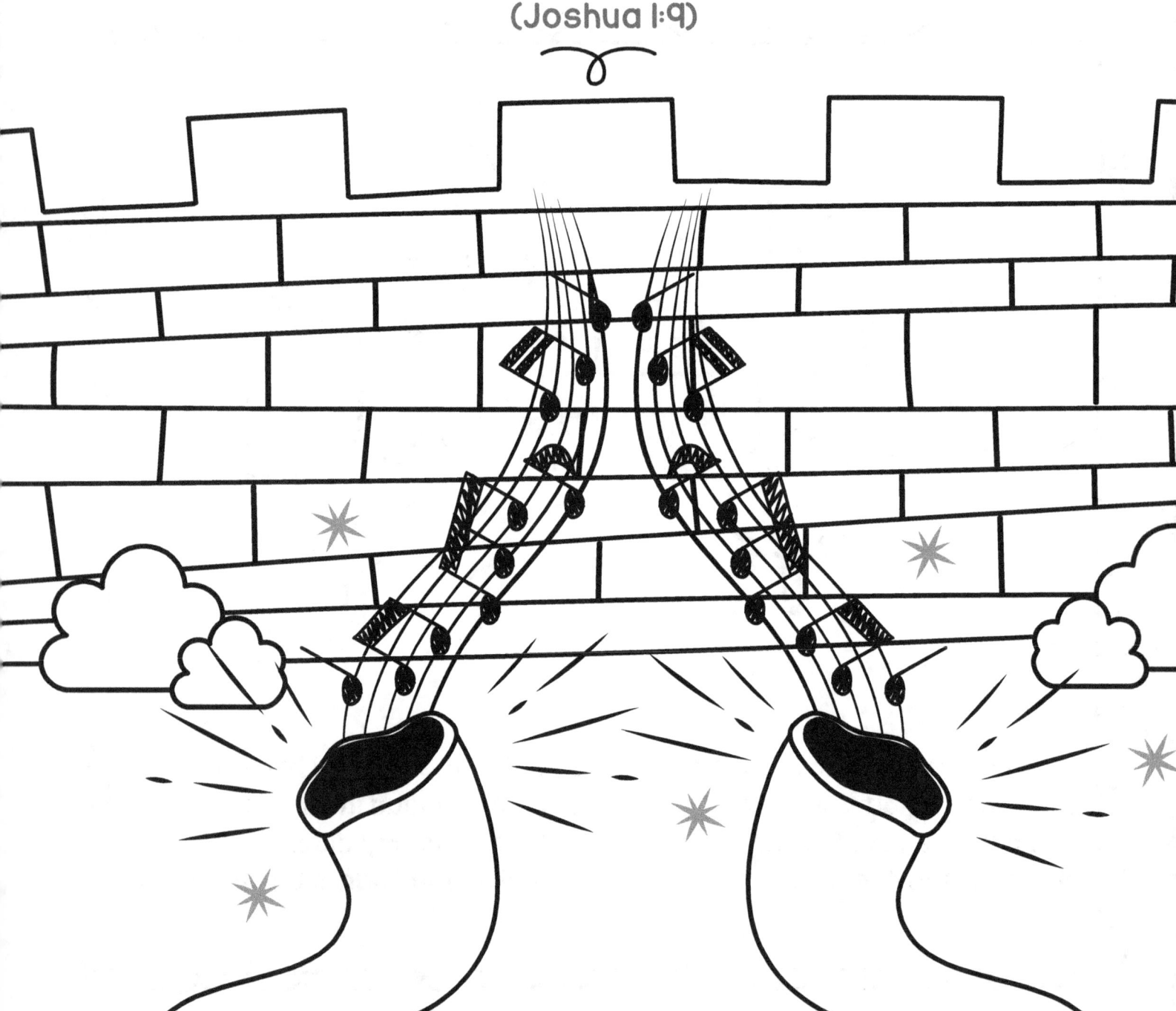

COURAGE

Courage is doing something, even when you feel afraid. God told Joshua to have courage (Joshua 1:9). Why do you think He said that? Do you think Joshua was afraid?

Draw something I am afraid of.

Draw how I show courage.

🌿 Make a shofar 🌿

Joshua told the priests to march around the city and blow the shofars. Let's make a shofar!

You will need:
1. Large paper plate
2. Construction paper
3. Tape and glue
4. Scissors (adults-only)
5. Paint, markers, ribbon, and yarn

Instructions:

1. Roll a large paper plate into a cone shape. Fasten with tape.
2. Glue construction paper around the cone shape. Use markers, ribbon or paint to decorate your 'shofar'.
3. Thread a piece of yarn through the inside of your shofar. Tie the ends to make a handle.

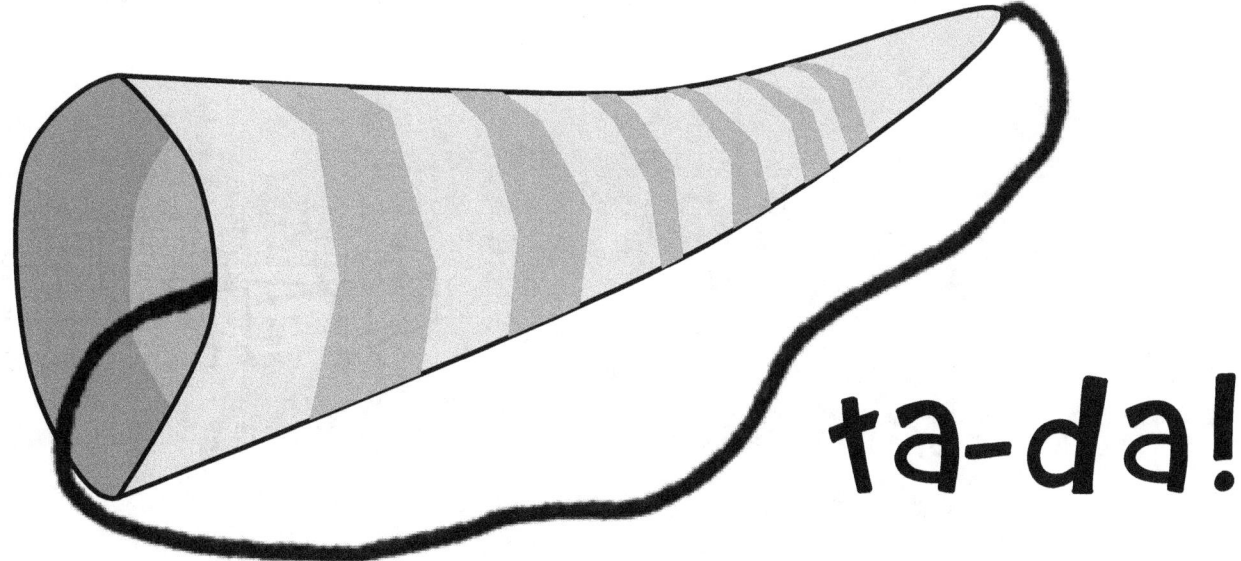

ta-da!

Fall of Jericho

Find and circle each of the words from the list below.

```
S F L U P S
C I T Y R H
Y E U B I O
N A R K E F
W A L L S A
S H O U T R
```

ARK   PRIEST
CITY   SHOFAR
WALL   SHOUT

What's different?

Circle the picture that is different.

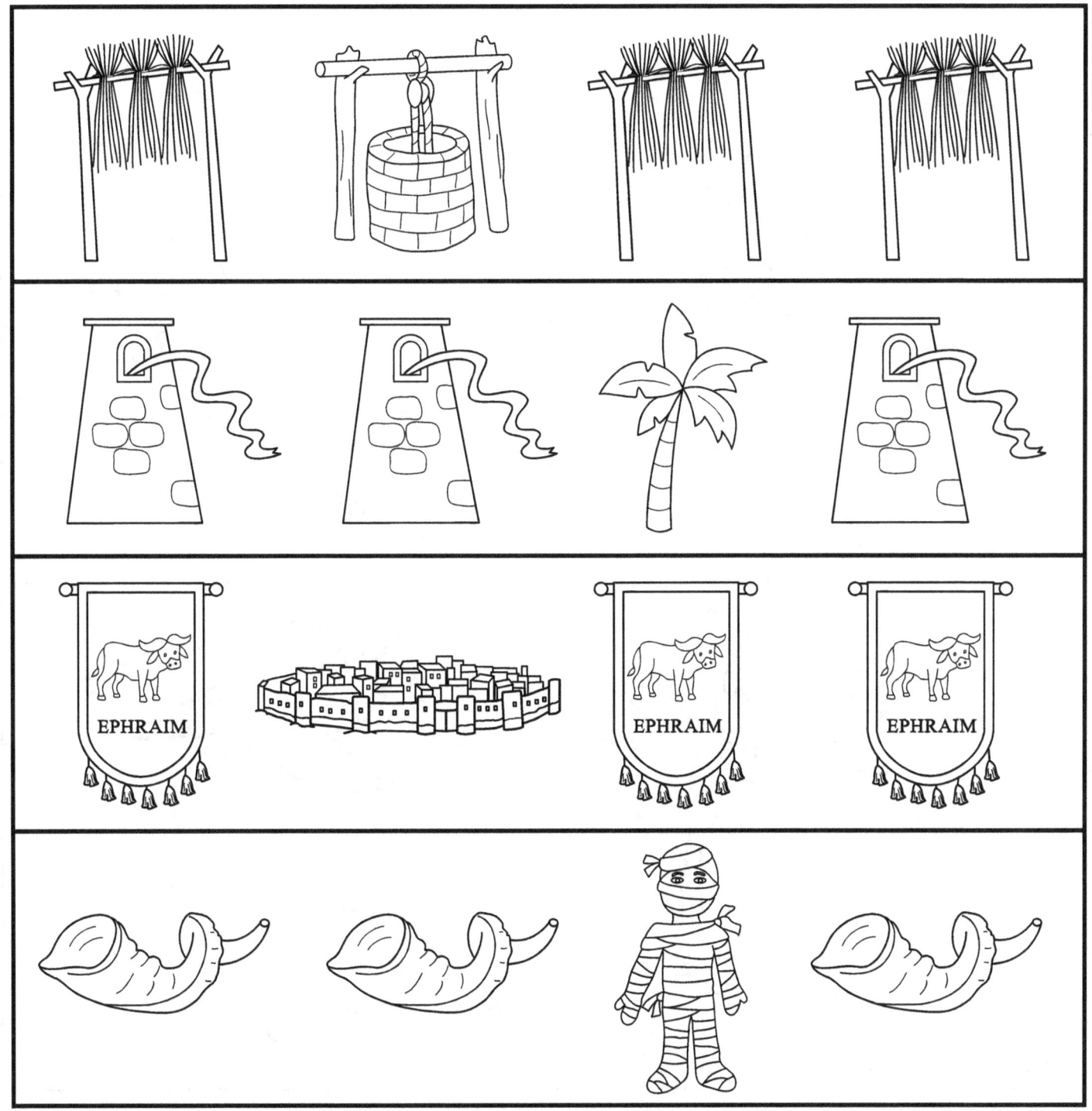

Up and down

The walls of Jericho fell <u>down</u> (Joshua 6:20).
The Israelites ran <u>up</u> into the city.
Circle the up picture and color the down picture.

R is for Rahab

The Israelites saved Rahab and her family (Joshua 6:23). Trace the letters. Color the picture.

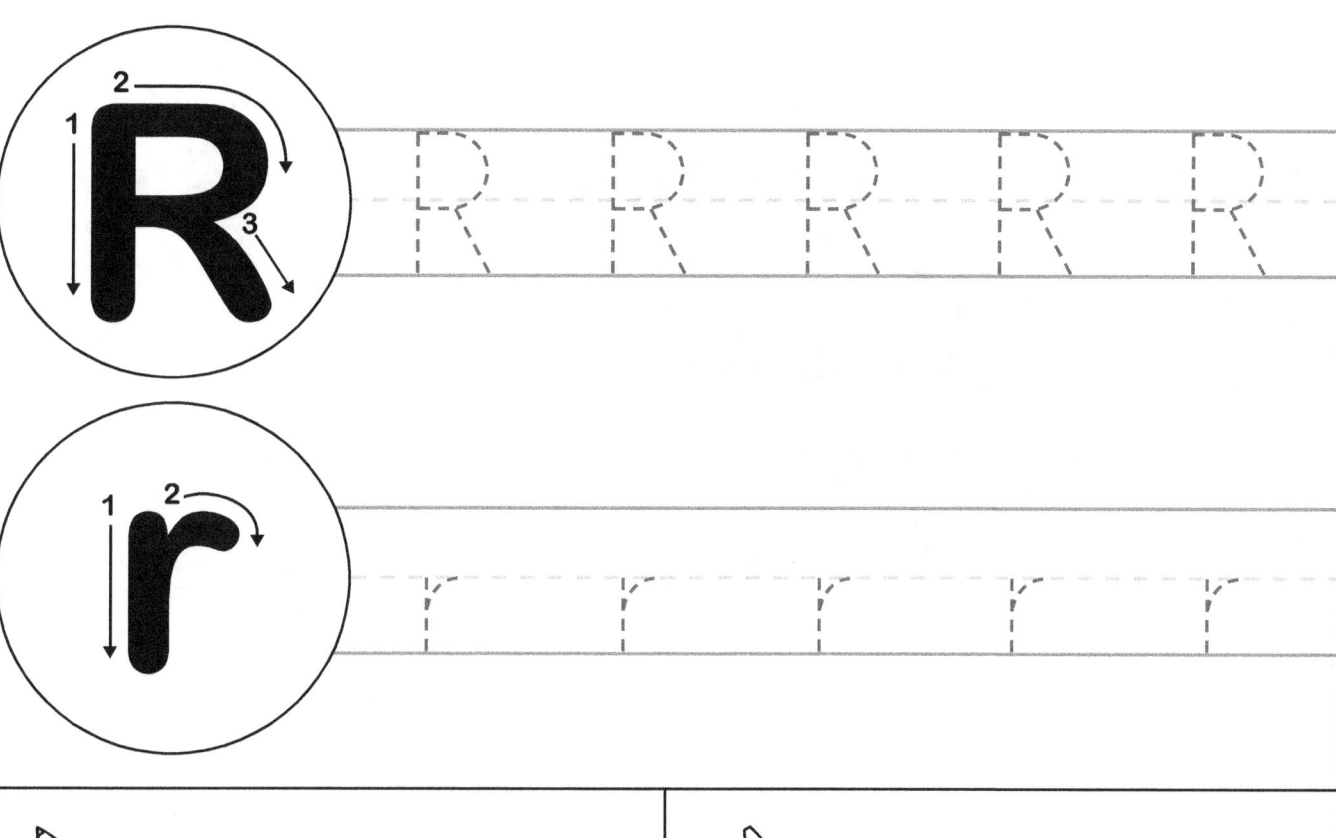

Trace the letter r

Color the Rahab

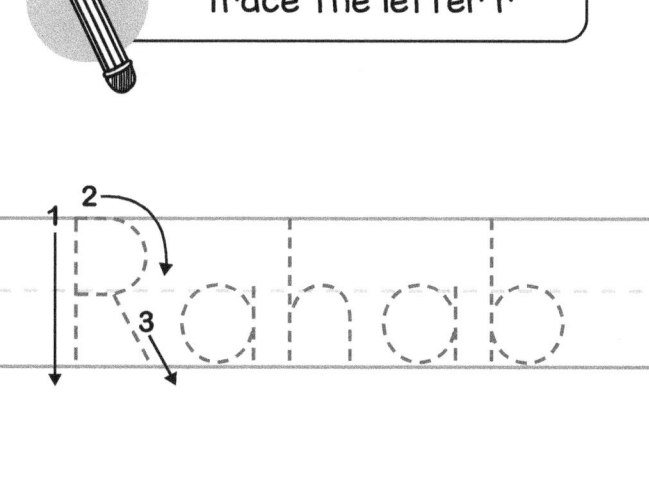

CRAFTS & PROJECTS

🌿 Let's make a menorah! 🌿

The Israelites made a golden menorah (lampstand) to put inside the tabernacle. Color and cut out your menorah and candles. Tape the candles to the menorah.

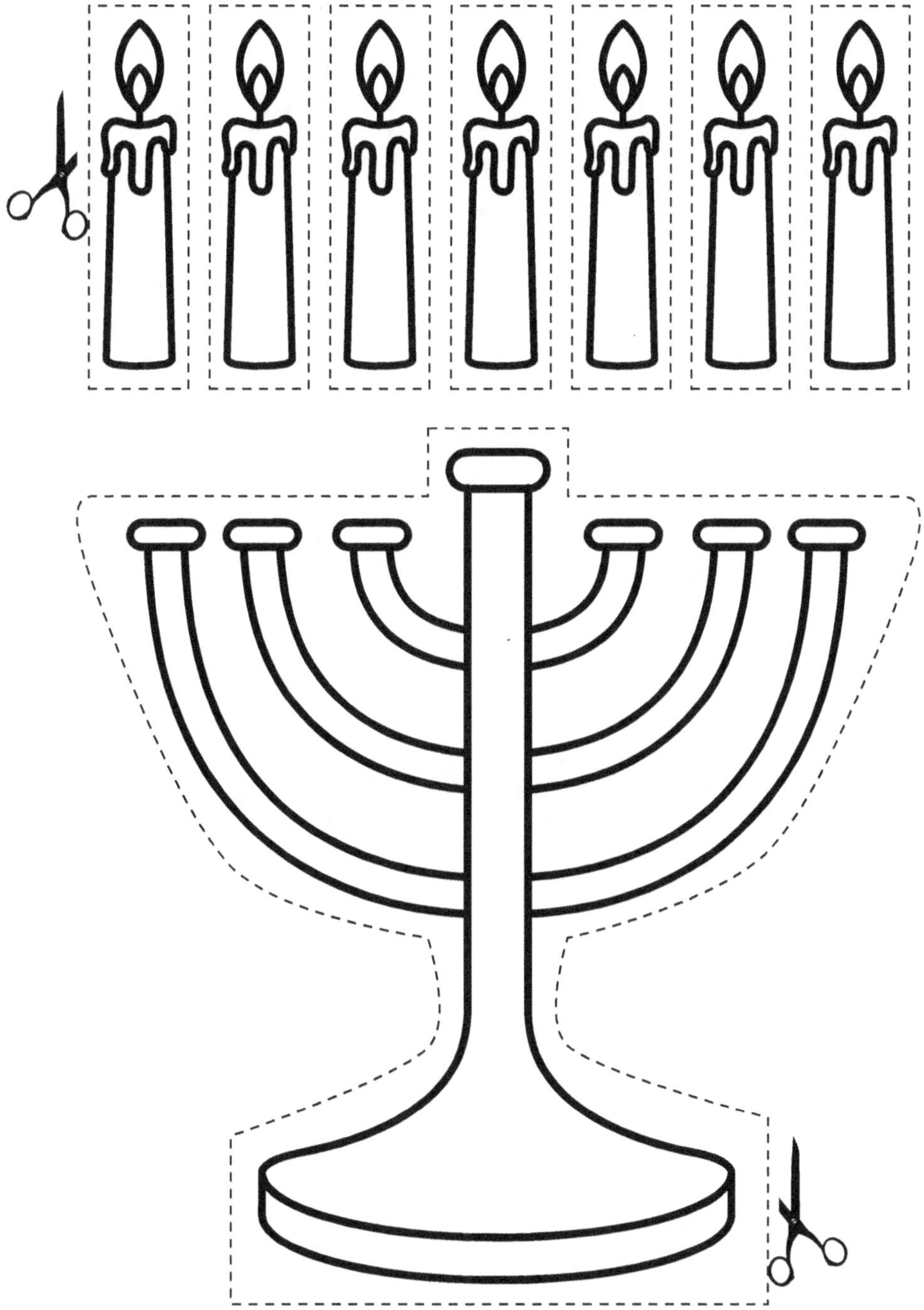

Flashcards

Color and cut out the flashcards.
Tape them around your home or classroom!

Tent

5

Flax

6

Ark of the Covenant
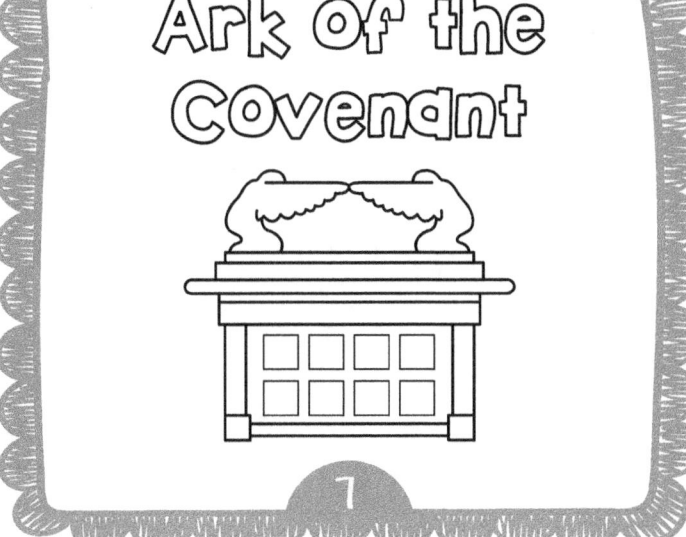
7

Rope

8

Walls of Jericho

Give each child a city wall template and pieces of colored paper. Ask them to paste the pieces of paper to build the walls of Jericho. On the next worksheet, ask them to draw what Jericho looked like after the walls fell down.

Teacher guide

 The Israelites lived in tents for forty years

 The Israelites made the ark of the covenant

 The spies hid under flax on Rahab's roof

 The spies escaped the city

 The Israelites crossed the river

 The Israelites ate the Passover

 The priests blew the shofars

 The walls of Jericho fell down

Retelling a story

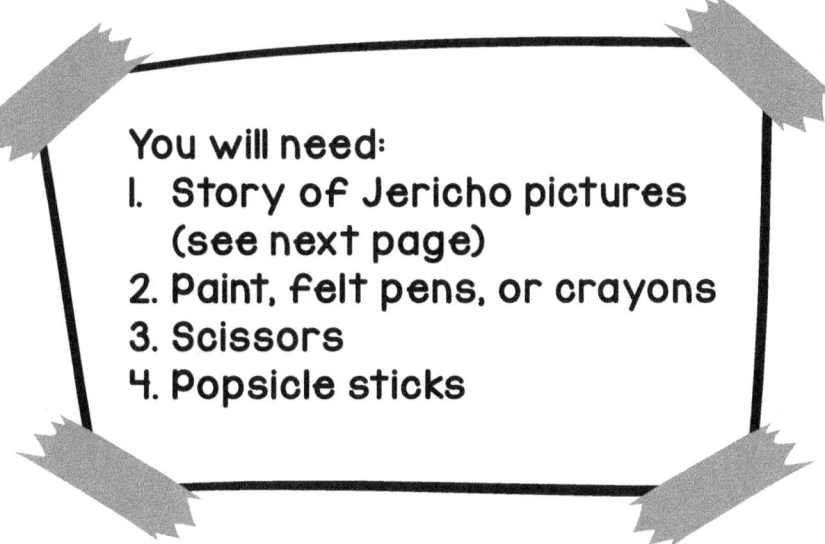

You will need:
1. Story of Jericho pictures (see next page)
2. Paint, felt pens, or crayons
3. Scissors
4. Popsicle sticks

Instructions:

1. Have your children color the pictures from the story of Battle of Jericho.
2. Cut out the pictures (children may need to help with this step).
3. Glue the circles onto popsicle sticks.
4. Use the sticks to help children retell the story of Joshua and the battle of Jericho. Refer to the Teacher Guide for a correct order of events.

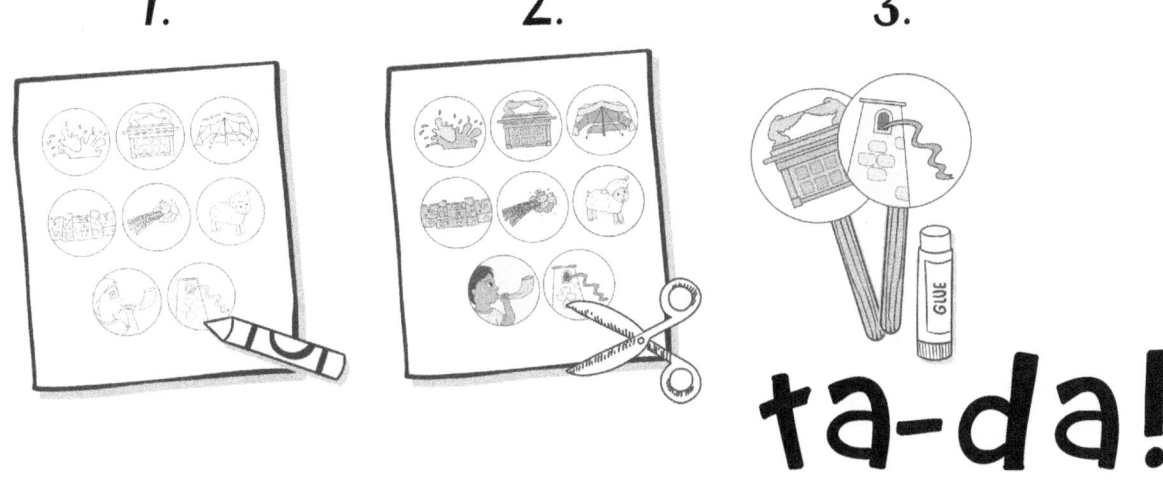

Certificate of Award

ANSWER KEY

Lesson One: To the promised land
Let's Review:
1. A new land – the land of Canaan
2. The Israelites lived in the desert for 40 years
3. Manna and quail, and water
4. The Israelites received God's laws at Mount Sinai, built a tabernacle, sent spies into Canaan, and fought their enemies (e.g. the Amalekites)
5. Moses was the Israelites' first leader, and Joshua was the Israelites' second leader

Bible word search puzzle: To the promised land…

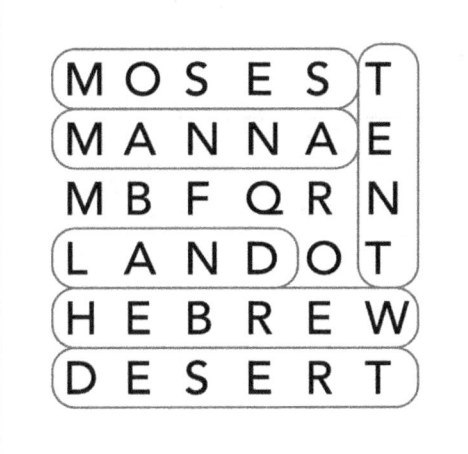

Lesson Two: Rahab and the spies
Let's Review:
1. Joshua needed a battle plan. He sent spies to Jericho to learn about the city
2. Rahab helped the spies
3. The spies hid under piles of flax on Rahab's roof
4. Tie a red rope to your window so we know who you are when we attack the city
5. The spies returned to the Israelite camp

Bible word search puzzle: Rahab and the spies

Lesson Three: Crossing the Jordan
Let's Review:
1. The Israelites were told to follow the priests
2. The Jordan River
3. Two parts
4. The Israelites built a memorial at the place where they camped
5. Twelve stones

Bible word search puzzle: Crossing the Jordan

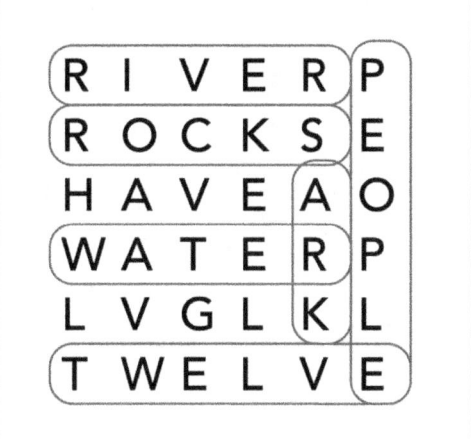

Lesson Four: Battle instructions
Let's Review:
1. The Passover meal
2. Manna from heaven
3. An angel (the commander of God's army)
4. Seven days
5. On the seventh day, the city walls will fall down and the Israelites can enter the city

Lesson Five: Battle of Jericho
Let's Review:
1. The ark of the covenant
2. Joshua told the people not to speak
3. The Israelites marched around the city wall seven times. The seventh time around, the priests blew their shofars and the Israelites shouted. The city wall fell down.
4. The two spies saved Rahab and her family
5. God was pleased with Joshua (Joshua 6:27)

Bible word search puzzle: Fall of Jericho

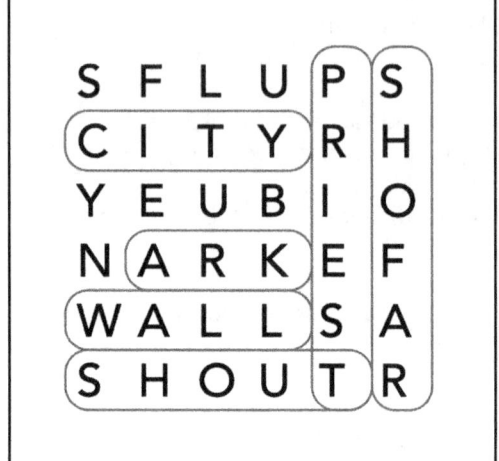

Discover more Activity Books!

Available for purchase at shop.biblepathwayadventures.com

INSTANT DOWNLOAD!

Battle of Jericho
Moses and the Ten Plagues (Beginners)
The Exodus (Beginners)
The story of Joseph (Beginners)

Learning Hebrew: The Alphabet
Favorite Bible Stories
The Spring Feasts
The Spring Feasts (Beginners)

www.ingramcontent.com/pod-product-compliance
Lightning Source LLC
Chambersburg PA
CBHW081311070526
44578CB00006B/839